· MEET ·
VINCENT VAN GOGH

Read With You Center for
Excellence in STEAM Education

Read With You

ISBN: 979-8-88618-080-0
First Edition January 2022

The Starry Night, 1889

Self-Portrait with a Straw Hat, 1887

The Bedroom, 1889

I went all over the Netherlands and painted the people and places I saw. What do you think is behind this blue man?

Houses and Figure, 1890

Café Terrace at Night, 1888

Vase with Twelve Sunflowers, 1888-1889

These flowers have quieter colors. Can you still find my brushstrokes?

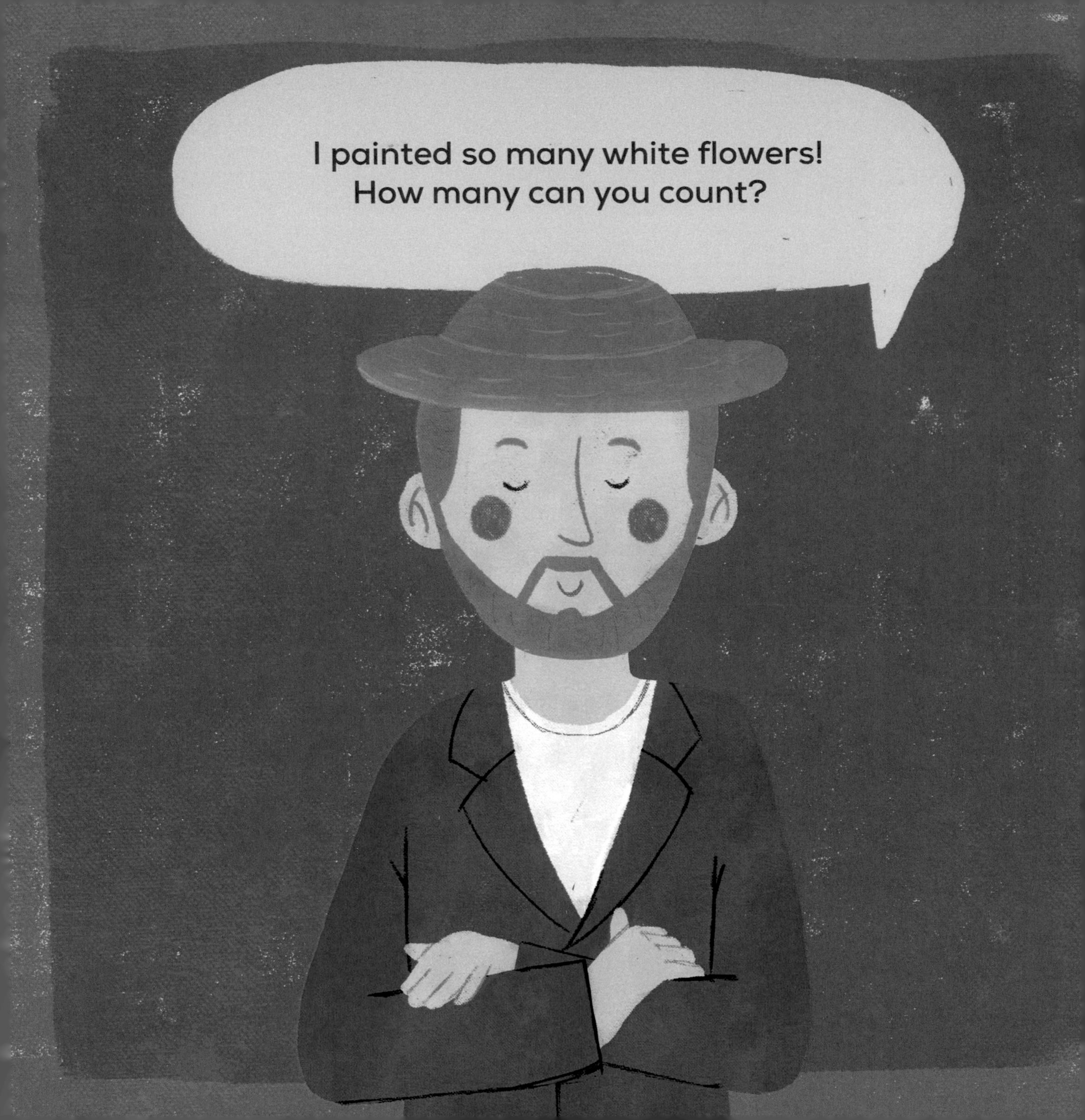
I painted so many white flowers!
How many can you count?

Almond Blossoms, 1890

The Siesta, 1890

Find Examples

Look at the picture on the next page and answer these questions.

Find the green color in the brown floor. Why do you think van Gogh mixed the green color in?

The pillows show curved lines. Trace the brushstrokes with your finger. How do you move your hand to make these lines?

The white and blue wall shows straighter brushstrokes. Trace them with your finger. How do you move your hand to make these lines?

Connect

This painting is titled *Irises* (1889).

Which lines in this painting are the curviest? Which lines are straighter?

Do the flowers look like real flowers? Why or why not?

If you could add one thing to the painting, what would you add?

What would you smell and hear if you were in this garden?

Craft

Option 1

1. Pick your favorite van Gogh drawing.

2. Look through your crayons or pencils. Find the colors that are closest to the colors in the drawing you picked.

3. Using just those colors, draw your own picture!

4. How can you mix the colors in fun ways?

Option 2

1. Find a picture of your favorite flowers online or in a book.

2. Using crayons or pencils, draw them in the same way van Gogh did. Use big, curvy lines and bright colors.

Made in the USA
Las Vegas, NV
23 October 2023

79465096R00024